The Water

Spirit

Kingdom

By

Debo Daniel

Published by Good News Ministries
220 Sleepy Creek Rd
Macon GA 31210

Table of Contents

DEDICATION

This book is dedicated to our God, Jehovah Sabaoth, the Lord of Hosts, the Man of War and the Commander of the Host who is willing and able to deliver all those who are under oppression of water spirits, individuals and nations alike.

ACKNOWLEDGMENTS

I appreciate and acknowledge the mentorship of the leaders of Intercessors for Nigeria in the persons of Barrister Emeka Nwakpa, Engineer Steve Olumuyiwa, Dr Kole Akinboboye, Dr Uduak Udofia and Engineer Ntiense Ubon Israel.

I also acknowledge the mentorship role of Dr John Robb, Director, World vision International. from whom I have learnt true servant leadership. Rev (Dr.) Moses Aransiola, I appreciate your mentoring role concerning my prayer life. You will not lose your reward.

Rev Mosy Madugba, you are a great blessing to me through your teachings and the annual International Ministers/ Christian Leaders Prayer Conference every January that sets me on fire.

Thank you for all your Godly counsel to me Rev. (Dr.) Reuben Ezemadu; Rev. (Dr.) I.D Lawon and Pastor (Dr.) U.A. Obed. I appreciate you. So much Dr. Tunde Oladoyinbo.

I wish to acknowledge my associates in ministry, Pastors Olugbenga Akande, Daniel Oluwalose, Kayode Peters Olaoba, Sola Mene, Solomon Sunday, Henry Hamilton,Goke Onasanya, Tunde Ojo all of whom labour closely and Tirelessly with me over Ibadan city. We shall see the travail of our souls over Ibadan city and we shall be satisfied. Thank you for always being there as a prayer shield for me in my numerous prophetic prayer warfare journeys.

Finally, I appreciate my partner in ministry, my helpmeet and my friend -my sweet wife Bimbo. Thanks for always being there to encourage and support me. The Lord will reward you.

AUTHOR

These are the days that the nations are raging and are imagining vain things, when the kings of the earth are setting themselves and the rulers are taking counsel together against the Lord and against His Anointed, saying, "Let us break their bonds in pieces and cast away their cords from us." And Jehovah Sabaoth, the Man of War who sits in the heavens, is laughing at their folly for they are fighting against their Creator. These are days the Lord shall speak to them in His wrath and vex them in His sore displeasure.

These are days that the Lord wants to teach principalities and power His manifold wisdom, the days Prophet Joel says:

"Proclaim this among the nations prepare for war wake up the mighty men let all the men of war draw near let them come up beat your plowshares into swords and your pruning hooks unto spears let the weak say 'I am strong.'" (**Joel 3:9-10**)

These are the days of Joshua and Caleb, Jehu, Gideon and Deborah Company-men and of valor who will go on the offensive against the kingdom of darkness to reclaim our lands for our soon coming KING so that the kingdoms of this world will become the kingdoms of our God and of His Christ.

These are days the church of God needs to deal decisively with the gods of the lands in order to reap large harvests of souls for our God who is fed up of people playing church, religious people who have a form of godliness but deny its power.

I believe God is "nauseated" with people who are not bold to confront the powers of darkness but will rather have social meetings in church without any manifestation of power

These are days God is searching for a company of people who will prepare the way of the LORD and make straight in the desert a highway for our GOD where every valley shall be exalted and every mountain and hill will be made low, crooked places will be made straight and rough places plain so that the glory of the LORD might be revealed.

These are days that the earth shall be filled with the knowledge of the glory of the LORD as the waters cover the sea.

These are days God is recruiting warriors who will refuse to entangle themselves with the affairs of this world that they might please Him who enlisted them as soldiers. He wants to give His warriors, treasures of darkness and hidden riches of secret places.

If you would like to be a part of this exciting company of warriors the LORD is raising in these last days, WELCOME ABOARD. We have the victory for the commander of the Host who has never and can never lose the battle, for the battle has been won 2,000 years ago on the cross of Calvary.

Debo Daniel, Author

CHAPTER 1

WATER IT

The importance of water to man cannot be overemphasized and this is why the Holy Spirit commissioned this assignment.

From the under-listed information, the reader will begin to understand how important water is to man and to God:

1. Before creation, the entire surface of the earth was covered with water. In other words, before the heavens and earth were created, all of creation was filled with water (**Gen. 1: 1-10**). Water existed before every other creation of God! It was from water that the earth was formed (**Gen. 1:8**) and the scriptures affirm that the whole earth was founded upon the waters.

"The earth is the LORD and the fulness thereof; the world, and they that dwell therein for He hath founded it upon the seas, and established it upon the floods." (**Ps. 24:1-2**).

2. Doctors and scientists confirm that 70% of human body weight consists of water.

3. 72% of present world surface is water.

4. Man needs water for everything. He can survive without food for up to two or three weeks but cannot survive without water for the same period. For man, water is needed for: Drinking, Bathing, Washing/General cleaning, Cooking, Farming, and Medicare in hospitals.

5. Water exists in the form of rains, streams, lakes, rivers and oceans.

6. The Bible also says the foundation of the whole earth is upon the waters.

"You who laid the foundations of the earth so that it should not be moved forever, you covered it with the deep as with a garment, the waters stood above the mountains." (**Ps. 104:5-6**)

7. God's throne itself is upon the waters. This shows the importance God himself attaches to water.

"The voice of the LORD is over the water; The God of glory thunders; The LORD is over many waters. The LORD sat enthroned at the Flood, and the LORD sits as King Forever." (**Ps. 29:3, 10**).

WARFARE TRANSFERRED INTO THE WATERS

God in His sovereignty and infinite wisdom gave so much prominence to water in creation as seen in the above-stated scriptures and information. Satan, on the other hand, who used to be the number one angel and who was created as Lucifer, is forever trying to copy and imitate the true things of God.

In his position as the number one angel, Lucifer was the ruler of the earth before the creation of man. He ruled the pre-Adamite world when there was no visible landmass, and the world was covered with water. It was for this reason that in the recreation, God said: "...and let the dry land appear..." (**Gen. 1:9**).

Then, Lucifer fell from this exalted position of being the number one angel, next to the Trinity through pride and rebellion. His fall is revealed in scriptures.

"How art thou fallen from heaven, O Lucifer, son of the morning! How art thou cut down to the ground, which didst weaken the nations! For thou hast said in thine heart, I will ascend into heaven, I will exalt my throne above the stars of God: I will sit also upon the mount of the congregation, in the sides of the north: I will ascend above the heights of the clouds; I will be like the most High. Yet thou shalt be brought down to hell, to the sides of the pit. They that see thee shall narrowly look upon thee, and consider thee, saying, Is this the man that made the earth to tremble, that did shake kingdoms; That made the world as a wilderness, and destroyed the cities thereof; that opened not the house of his prisoners?" (**Is 14 12-17**).

"And He [Jesus] said unto them, I beheld Satan as lightning fall from heaven." (**Luke 10:18**).

"And another sign appeared in heaven: behold, a great, fiery red dragon having seven heads and ten horns, and seven diadems on his heads.... And there was war in heaven. Michael and his angels fought against the dragon, and the dragon and his angels fought and war broke out in heaven: Michael and his angels fought with the dragon; and the dragon and his angels fought, but they did not prevail, nor was a place found for them in heaven any longer. So the great dragon was cast out, that serpent of old, called the Devil and Satan, who deceives the whole world; he was cast to the earth, and his angels were cast out with him." (**Revelation 12: 3, 7-9**).

Again, the fall of Lucifer was expressed in **Ezekiel 28: 12-19**. When Lucifer had fallen and had been cast out of heaven, he was overthrown and cast into the earth and the seas. At his overthrow, the host of heaven declared in a loud voice.

"*Rejoice, O heavens, and you who dwell in them! Woe to the inhabitants of the earth and the sea! For the devil has come down to you, having great wrath,because he knows that he has a short time.*" (**Rev 12:12**, emphasis mine).

Heavens rejoiced, but that began the problem for the earth and the seas because the one who troubled them in heaven had been cast to the earth and the seas!

Since he had been overthrown, Satan, meaning adversary, had been attempting to thwart and stop God's plan to bring peace unto His kingdom.

After the first prophecy in **Genesis 3:15** that God will use the seed of the woman to bruise the head of Satan and destroy his kingdom, he (Satan) began to look for the Man that fulfills the prophecy so as to destroy Him.

The first attempt was to try and pollute the human race through fallen angels whom he commissioned to assume the form of humans and marry women. This was to destroy the seed of mankind (**Gen. 6**) by introducing the sins of fornication, idolatry and homosexuality. This "satanically-induced marriage" succeeded in producing giants through sexual intercourse between these fallen angels and women on earth.

However, God had a remnant in Noah who was not corrupted.. Through Noah and his righteousness, God was able to preserve His plan to redeem the earth from the dark kingdom. Through Noah God preserved a remnant (eight people) in the entire human race. Again, Satan tried desperately to pollute and destroy the human race through the sins of drunkenness and cursing, but God preserved a remnant in Abram, established a covenant with him and brought the Messiah, Jesus Christ through his lineage. The complete genealogy of Jesus was traced in Matthew 1. The main purpose why Jesus came is to do the will of His father and to destroy the works of the Dark Kingdom (**1 Jn. 3:8**).

Now, all power and authority in heaven and earth is still vested in Christ Jesus but it is to be manifested through His body, the church. This is the day and age when His body should arise from slumber and begin to exercise authority offensively over the kingdom of darkness.

We are not supposed to be harassed by the devil and be on the defensive but since our master, Jesus Christ came to destroy the works of the devil, we ought to be an army aggressively raiding and destroying the dark kingdom in our lives, in the lives of our family members and relations, in our communities, cities and our world.

Jesus assured us and said, "The gates of hell shall not prevail against the Church." (**Matt 16:18**). When Jesus said, "I will give you the keys of the kingdom of Heaven." He was saying to the Church, "You will have all the available resources in Heaven at your disposal."

Would Jesus have said this if He wanted us to eagerly struggle through life and merely look forward to the rapture as a means of escape from the world?

No! He expects us to enforce His victory by exercising the authority He has given us to defeat Satan in our lives and in our world, so that the kingdoms of this world might become the kingdoms of our God and of His Christ.

BACK TO THE INFLUENCE OF WATERS

With 72% of the earth's surface covered by water, Satan decided in his rebellion to build his power base in the waters. His "secretariat" is in the heavenlies where the powers and principalities supervise satanic oppression of territories, cities and nations but his "operational base" is in the waters.

Since the foundation of the earth is on the water (**Ps. 104:5-6**) and the whole earth was founded upon the waters (**Ps. 24:1-2**), Satan also decided the best place to pitch his kingdom's power base is in the waters, because he likes to counterfeit everything God does.

CHAPTER 2

WATER SPIRITS IN THE SCRIPTURES

All through scriptures, we see the operation of Satan and his dark forces from the waters and it is only an undiscerning believer that will say there is nothing like water spirits.

1. Satan himself came out of the sea in Revelation 13.

"Then I stood on the sand of the sea. And I saw a beast rising up out of the sea, having seven heads and ten horns, and on his horns ten crowns, and on his heads a blasphemous name."

In verses 6 and 7 of Revelation 13, we read how the beast opened his mouth speaking great things and blasphemies against God to blaspheme His name, His tabernacle and those who dwell in heaven. In verse 7, the Bible says, "It was granted to him to make war with the saints and to overcome them."

This is why we believe the power base of Satan is in the waters.

2. God asked Moses to "Go to Pharaoh in the morning when he goes out to the water and you shall stand by the river's bank to meet him..."(**Ex. 7:15**).

What would a powerful king like Pharaoh be doing by the river's side in the morning? I will tell you, he went to acquire power from the water spirits for the day, the same way believers ought to receive strength and direction for the day from God through their quiet time.

In the first of ten plagues that God used to deal with all the gods of Egypt, He demonstrated His power over Khnum, the ram god who was the supposed protector of the source of the Nile and Hapy, the god of the Nile. By this spiritual warfare against the water spirits of the Nile, God dealt with them and killed all the fish by turning the water into blood and the Egyptians could not get water to drink for the next seven days. The river stank and there was blood all over Egypt.

This was God's way of dealing with the water spirits upon which Pharaoh depended for strength.

3. Jesus understood the manifestation of water spirits. There are occasions when they bring about raging storms in the sea and unless people discern their manifestation and exercise their authority to rebuke them, they cause tragedy and death.

The Reubenites, Gadites and half the tribe of Manasseh who refused to cross over to Canaan occupied the country of the Gadarenes (**Num. 32:2-5, 33**).

As Jesus crossed over, a furious storm arose as water spirits were trying to overturn the boat.

In their natural state, trees, rocks, water, etc., give glory to God (**Ps. 148**). They will not normally challenge the authority of Jesus.

Whilst the disciples were crying that they were perishing, Jesus exercised kingdom authority (which He has now given us through the Holy Spirit), and rebuked the spirit behind the wind and the sea (**Matt. 8:26**).

But He said to them "'Why are you fearful O you of little faith?'" Then He arose and rebuked the winds and the sea and there was great calm.

If it was a natural godly storm, Jesus will not rebuke something that is from His father. He knew the storm was an evil manifestation of water spirits.

It is also reasonable to conclude that water spirits possessed the Gardarene demon-possessed men that met Him as soon as He came out of the boat on the other side because:

They recognized who Jesus was.

They pleaded through the Garderene demoniacs that Jesus should cast them out into the herd of swine.

They caused the herd of swine to run violently into the sea (**Matt. 8:32**) In the natural, pigs hate water; it was the water spirits that chased them into the water and killed them.

These spirits are normally violent spirits that do not let go of their captives easily. (**Mark 5:1-13**)

As demonic forces manipulate the winds, so also dark forces operating from the waters influence the water to do evil. The swine perished in the waters but the water spirits went back into their habitat, the sea.

Water spirits normally put up great resistance in deliverance but ultimately bow to the name of Jesus and the anointing (**Mark 4:35-41; Matt. 8:23-32**).

4. Job was complaining bitterly to his friends and to God after his affliction and suffering and said at one point, *"Am I a sea or a sea serpent that you set a guard over me?"* (**Job 7:12**).

Job understood that there is a demonic force called "sea serpent" that basically is a water spirit.

5. Leviathan: This was a massive sea creature that the Bible says: God created to play in the sea (**Ps. 104:26**). It is so massive it has no fears of harassment by human fishermen.

However, it was corrupted by Satan to become an evil creature and thus an enemy of God.

"You divided the sea by your strength; You broke the heads of the sea serpents in the waters. You broke the heads of Leviathan in pieces, and gave him as food to the people inhabiting the wilderness" (**Ps. 74:13-14**).

Here, the Psalmist was referring to the deliverance of Israel from Egypt, how God divided the Red sea for His people to pass through on dry ground, but how He had to break the head of Leviathan to execute the deliverance. Friend, operation of Satan from the waters is real!

Also, Isaiah released God's judgment on Leviathan by the great and strong sword of the Lord.

"In that day, the Lord with His severe sword, great and strong, will punish Leviathan, the fleeing serpent, Leviathan, that twisted serpent and He will slay the reptile that is in the sea." (**Is. 27:1**).

The Lord was asking Job questions as to his strength and ability using the strength and power of Leviathan as a measure, God says, *"Can you draw out Leviathan with a hook, or snare his tongue with a line which you lower? Can you put a reed through his nose, or pierce his jaw with a hook?"* (**Job 41:1-10a**).

No one is so fierce that they will dare stir him up. Leviathan is a demon principality operating against ministries and whole cities and nations.

God was asking that if Job cannot play with such a massive sea creature, can he stand against Him, the one who created Leviathan?

In **Job 3:8**, the Bible refers to powerful occultists who use the Leviathan for their evil deeds, i.e., to pronounce curses and to influence people's lives.

"May those who curse days, curse that day, those who are ready to rouse Leviathan."

6. Water Spirits arc referred to as Rahab. In Psalm 89, the water spirits were referred to as Rahab,

"You rule the raging of the sea when its waves rise, you still them you have broken Rahab in pieces as one who is slain, you have scattered your enemies with your mighty arm" **(Ps 89:9-10)**.

These verses linked up with **Psalm 87: 4** and **Isaiah 30:7** all point to the fact that Rahab here refers to the power behind Egypt which is the water spirits, the spirits Pharaoh went to fellowship with and draw power from every morning.

7. When God asked prophet Ezekiel to prophesy judgment against Pharaoh king of Egypt and against all Egypt, He compared Pharaoh to a great monster that lies in the midst of the rivers.

"Son of man, set your face against Pharaoh king of Egypt, and prophesy against him, and against all Egypt. Speak, and say, 'GOD: Behold, I am against you, O Pharaoh king of Egypt, O great monster that lies in the midst of his rivers, Who has said, my River is my own; I have made it for myself.'" **(Ezek. 29:2-3)**.

By covenant with these waters, Pharaoh had imbibed their character, secondly, in **Job 9:13** (NKJV), the Bible says, "*God will not withdraw His anger the allies of the proud He prostrates beneath Him.*" (**Job 9:13**).

In NKJV Rahab is translated by the word proud but a reference or margin is given explaining that the proud is translated from the Hebrew word Rahab. In NIV, the word Rahab is maintained.

God does not restrain His anger, even the cohort of Rahab cowered at His feet. (**Job 9: 13**).

This means that God is angry against Rahab and His anger cannot be stopped, and that the allies of Rahab are also dealt with by God.

Thirdly, in **Job 26:12-13** (NIV), the Bible says, "*By His power, He churned up the sea; By His wisdom, He cut Rahab to pieces; By His breadth, the skies became fair; His hand pierced the gliding serpent.*"

Again, the scriptures were referring to God's judgment and dealing with Rahab in verse 12 and Leviathan in verse 13.

The Rahab in all these scriptures is definitely not the prostitute called by the same name in Joshua chapter 2 who lived in the city of Jericho, but rather, a sea monster or water spirit, a principality.

CHAPTER 3

ATTRIBUTES AND CHARACTERISTICS OF WATER SPIRITS

The water spirit arm of the kingdom of darkness exhibits certain attributes and characteristics which are common to people, places and cities where there is apparent manifestation or presence of these spirits.

1. Excessive pride and arrogance, manifesting in self-confidence, critical attitude towards others, total independence, desiring to be served, desire to be honored, desire to control others, boasting over achievements and dishonoring constituted authority.

"Because your heart is lifted up and you say I am a god and I seat in the of gods, in the midst of the sea...And your heart is lifted up because of your riches" (**Ez. 28:2-5**).

"...My river is my own, I made it for myself." (**Ez. 29:3b**).

Pharaoh arrogated to himself the power of creation and of being a god. (See also, **1 Cor. 8:5-6.**)

2. Homes and marriages are affected resulting in broken homes and marriages.

3. Difficulty for people to get married and stay married

4. "Churches" of error operate in areas where there is manifestation of water spirits.

5. They attack God's work and God's servants and unless God's grace helps the servants, they fall into sexual sins or into heresy. In many coastal or riverime areas, we have seen many Holiness preachers trapped by sexual sins and falling into such sins. Promiscuity, juvenile delinquency, immorality and prostitution are common sins where they operate.

6. They lock up people's material wealth and fortunes in the waters (**Nah. 2:6**).

7. They cause sexual abuse in dreams to those who are under their influence and they see themselves swimming in dreams or bathing by the rivers, etc.

8. Men and women that have water spirit problems find it difficult to be spiritually strong because of attacks from the water-attacks on their spiritual growth, i.e., prayer, Bible study.

9. They reveal secrets to their worshipers and that's why their worshipers see "visions" and are involved in divination. (**Ezek 28:3**).

10. Kings and traders have gained riches by the wisdom given them by water spirits (**Ezek. 28:4**).

11. They cause delay and difficulties in conception.

12. Loss of desire for spouse because they have sex in dreams with their spirit spouses in the spirit.

13. They cause people to love pleasures excessively.

14. They promote sorceries, enchantments and divination (Nah. 3:1-4). They constitute a powerful level of witchcraft (**Deut. 18:10-11**).

15. They manifest violence because they are violent spirits, i.e., the spirits in the Gardarene demoniacs were responsible for driving the swine violently down the steep into the sea and drowning them (**Mark 5:7-13**). Nineveh was situated by the sea and was reported to be a bloody war-like and violent city (**Nahum 3:1-3**).

16. They impact on people the tendency to go nude, i.e., this is the spirit behind people who walk naked on nude beaches. They alter the personality of people they inhabit, i.e., a normally decent person will see nothing wrong in walking around nude, even at the beach.

17. Water spirits bring evil characteristics into kings and presidents and through them into cities and nations-pride, pollution, terror, wickedness and immorality. In other words, they rule and govern whole nations which are under their influence through manipulation of the presidents and other political leaders.

18. Water Spirits manifesting as Leviathan also manifest these effects on people:

Insanity, paralysis, schizophrenia and other illnesses

Discord, strife and accusation

Chaos and suffering

Proud, haughty, condescending, and arrogant attitude.

Stubborn, cold-hearted

Lack of concentration, learning difficulties

Gloominess and depression

Unteachable, judgmental, possessive and legalistic

Seeks to control and associated with Jezebel spirit

Independent attitude, excessive self- confidence

Deafness and blindness to the Holy spirit, counterfeit ministries and worship

Miscommunication, deception, twisting the truth, lying, gossip and slander.

Dishonoring of authority.

(Culled from Amanda Buys, The Four Elements: Earth, Air, Fire and Water)

19. Since their objective is to prevent mankind from worshiping the true God, the creator of the universe, they deceive people through worldly philosophies (**Col. 2:8**) and through false religion and all kinds of cults (**Col. 2:18**).

20. They strengthen themselves through human blood and so they use many devises like air, road and water accidents, sickness, ritual killing, wars and other means by which they shed blood.

21. They use material and financial resources to manipulate their devotees: *"Bow before me and I will make you rich"* and many have bowed to them to serve them. They have by their wisdom monopolized and cornered a lot of the world's materials resources, and they flaunt these to enslave undiscerning people.

"With your wisdom and understanding you have gained riches for yourself and gathered gold and silver into your treasuries. By your great wisdom in trade, you have increased your riches and your heart is lifted up because of your riches." (**Ezek. 28:4-5**).

CHAPTER 4

MANIFESTATIONS OF WATER SPIRITS

How they are worshiped?

There are many ways people invoke the power of water spirits through worship. Some of them are listed hereunder:

1. On the beachfronts of many African nations, we find members of certain religious sects always having their worship and spending days and nights "praying" into the sea. Usually they are attired in white gowns and burn candles. Examples of this can be found in Bar Beach in Lagos Nigeria and Monrovia Beach in Liberia.

2. Bathing in ponds or rivers at certain times of the day (midnight or midday); this ritual bath is "baptism" into water spirit worship

3. Throwing objects like clothes, jewelry, underwear or beads inside the waters or leaving such items like chicken, goats or other livestock as sacrifice near the river or streams as directed by the water spirit priests or priestesses

4. Sprinkling of "holy" waters on devotees

5. Purification rituals involving the washing of hands and feet and sex organs of devotees in sacred streams and rivers

6. Fetish priests take young girls to the river to batheg them and marry them to the water spirits making scarifies to the spirits. Usually such girls become prostitutes and lesbians and find it extremely difficult to marry or to keep their marriage.

7. In the riverine areas of some countries in Africa, a new baby is dropped into a river on their day of birth and collected seven days later. If he dies, that means he is "unacceptable" to the river gods but if he lives, the gods have accepted him or her. This is a dedication of the baby to the water spirits.

8. Some "white garment" sects usually build their "churches" near rivers deriving their power from the waters.

9. Wombs can become water-spirit altars when a woman is asked to go and wash in a certain river before she can conceive.

10. In many coastal areas, fishermen make sacrifices to these spirits in order to have a good catch. Some also sacrifice to their nets.

11. In Haiti, there is a waterfall where voodooists from all over the world come on annual pilgrimage and offer worship to the water spirits to receive greater voodoo

power. The devotees drop all kinds of tokens around the waterfalls and in the waters. These are covenant tokens with water spirits.

12. In India, there are sacred rivers like the Ganges where people go in to wash at specific periods of the year and offer sacrifices of various objects.

13. In many cities in the western world, fountains are created and people are asked to drop coins inside the fountains and make a wish. This is water spirit worship. The coins are a covenant token making a covenant with the water spirit.

14. In a city called Venice, 30 minutes away from Santa Monica, California, there is a beachfront where there is much apparent occult activity. It is like a market or exhibition center of Satan, where virtually every occult group is represented, marketing their spiritual wares.

15. Forbidding to fish on certain days or at certain seasons is another manifestation of water spirit worship or in some cases; it is forbidden to fish in sacred streams and rivers.

16. Festivals like Osun Osogbo in South West Nigeria, where tens of thousands of people from all over Nigeria and abroad come together once a year to worship the river goddess called Osun Osogbo, the goddess of River Osogbo.

17. Serpents come out of the waters (rivers or seas) that the people worship and in return the serpents do not bite them. The worshipers even play with the serpents from the waters in some cases. Some devotees have sex with the serpents.

18. People who have been set free from deep involvement in the kingdom of darkness and who are now in Christ Jesus have testified to the reality of a kingdom under the sea from where Satan is said to control his followers in the world. It is the strategic operational control center of the kingdom of darkness.

19. Many kings and presidents of nations (like Pharaoh of Egypt in **Ex. 7:15**) go to raise altars at the source of many rivers to draw strength from water spirits, to secure power to rule. In the case of some big rivers in Africa some of which run through more than one nation, kings and presidents raise marine altars at the source of such rivers and derive witchcraft power for their oppressive rule from such worship of water spirit. Some African presidents are known to have raised such altars at the source of River Nile and hence they rule in wickedness by evil power from water spirits, i.e., an ex-strongman of Democratic Republic of Congo (DRC) in Africa (then called Zaire) worked closely with water spirits and institutionalized sorcery as an act of government to control the nation and its wealth.

20. Mariners pour libation into the sea as a covenant with water spirits to ensure safe voyages at sea and fishermen do same to ensure a good harvest of fish.

21. Important landmark areas and places in cities with water spirit manifestations have such places named to glorify the spirit, e.g., a restaurant in a big hotel was named "MERMAID RESTAURANT."

22. In many countries in Asia and Africa, before bridges are built over rivers, the rivers are appeased with blood sacrifice. This in effect is appeasing the water spirits that are believed to be controlling the waters. There is a beach on the Atlantic seashore in Lagos, Nigeria and each time there is a ocean surge and it overflows the boundaries onto the city, the water spirit priests claim the water goddess is angry and needs to be appeased with animal sacrifice.

23. Some kings or traditional rulers have to go through some ritual baths before completing their requirements of the initiations necessary before they ascend the throne to govern. This is not an ordinary bath.

24. Initiation into manhood rituals is still carried out in certain communities and this involves taking such candidates to certain sacred stream or rivers for ritual baths and "cleansing" some communities in Africa, during puberty, water spirit priests take nubile maidens to rivers or steams where older women or the water spirit priestesses bathe them.

25. On the full moon every November in Thailand, little boats called Putons decorated with flowers are put on the rivers to carry away the troubles of people as they float downstream. People expect better things to come after this ritual, which is a combined worship of the moon goddess and water spirits. It happens during the LOIKOTONG festival. (Culled from Idolatry: Emeka Nwakpa, page 114.)

26. Water spirits also manifest as Mermaids having the head of a woman but the tail of a fish instead of legs (see picture on front cover). The Merman's have the head of a man but the tail of fish instead of legs. According to Encyclopedia Britannia, Vol. 15, page 196, mermaids and mermen are members of a cultural race half human and half-fish; they inhabit the sea and some inland waters, though they can also live on land. Some live on both land and water while others live in stones and rocks, some in trees and others in all kinds of waters, etc.

These are only a few manifestation of the worship of water spirits. Many of the above stated examples involve covenants with the marine spirits and raising of marine altars to worship them.

Whoever reads this and still denies the existence or reality of water spirits needs to ask God to please open his spiritual eyes, as Elisha asked God for his servant in **2 Kings 6:15-17**. Please stop and read this passage.

CHAPTER 5

HOW PEOPLE AND TERRITORIES ARE CONTAMINATED, INFESTED, INITIATED AND OPPRESSED BY THE WATER SPIRITS

People and territories are contaminated, infested, initiated and oppressed by the water spirits in the following ways:

1. Through initiation by parents or ancestors by reason of one's family lineage

2. Through the geographical location a man lives or where he is born. Even when you do not consciously invite the water spirits, as long as they are ruling spirits in their environment, a person can get contaminated/infested as long as he is not in Christ and even if he or she is but does not have understanding of deliverance or spiritual warfare (**Hos. 4:6; Is. 5:13-14**).

3. Through sexual sins, i.e., adultery, fornication, incest, homosexuality, rape, masturbation, lesbianism, and bestiality; all of these open doors for water spirit demonization.

4. Through involvement in feasts, festivals, rituals and satanic initiations many of which are done in ignorance in the name of culture or tradition, i.e., the place in

Africa where they have a tradition of dropping newborn babies into the water and picking them up in seven days.

5. Through names given to individuals.

6. Through marriage to those who are already infested or initiated.

7. For pregnant women who are asked to go and have a bath in the sea and drop things into the water, they have unwittingly initiated that baby in the womb.

8. For women who need the fruit of the womb and they are asked to bath in the river, the child they will conceive has been dedicated and initiated from the womb.

9. Some "pastors" seeking satanic power visit the seashore, are asked to make certain incantations, and thereafter are "admitted" into the water spirit world through an opening into the water. Thereafter, they manifest "power" and "wealth", but they are not from the God of Abraham, Isaac and Jacob.

10. Some get infested with water spirits by reason of artifacts they buy and decorate their homes with or dedicated clothes and jewelry they adorn their bodies with; pictures and or paintings of mermaid (the head of a woman with the tail of a fish) these constitute an altar of water spirits and do contaminate.

11. Dropping sacrifices into farmland, ponds, rivers, streams, lakes, oceans or placing them by the side of any of these bodies of water results in invitation

12. Tossing coins into water bodies and making a wish with such actions result in infestation with water spirits because this is indirectly invoking them to work for the person

13. Through divination and enchantments released on the undiscerning

14. Through eating food cooked by people possessed by water spirits of course without giving thanks to sanctify the food, e.g., an evangelist who used to be a high-level occultist claimed in his testimony he got initiated into witchcraft through fried bean-balls.

15. Through naming streets and towns after water spirits, i.e., dedicating such places to these spirits, e.g., Popo Yemoja in Ibadan, Nigeria, meaning Water Spirit Street.

16. Through sexual involvement with those who are "carriers" of water spirits.

17. Through visiting herbalists for power or protection.

18. Through visiting marine spirit priests out of curiosity or just being adventurous.

This list is not comprehensive, as the devil is subtle in the way he deceives people and gets them initiated into his kingdom.

WHY PEOPLE GET INITIATED

People have a myriad of reasons for entering into covenant with spirits. A few of such reasons include:

1. Desire for power to rule.

2. To possess magical powers.

3. To get healed of sicknesses and afflictions.

4. To have children when this had been difficult or impossible.

5. To gain wealth and riches.

6. To exercise powers of witchcraft.

7. To ensure safe voyage on the seas.

8. To ensure a good catch of fish, lobsters and other edible sea animals.

9. To get rain and a good harvest in agriculture.

10. To have access to supernatural power.

11. In order to establish thrones and stools and acquire power to win battles and wars.

12. To serve for themselves protection from affliction, danger and death.

13. To get "delivered" from demonic oppression.

14. In order to succeed in their endeavors.

People who get initiated for these reasons lack understanding, and it is only a relationship with Jesus Christ that can set them free.

CHAPTER 6

THE NEED TO DO WARFARE AGAINST WATER SPIRITS AND HOW!

From the foregoing chapters, it is evident that the water-spirit kingdom is a very important arm of the kingdom of darkness of Satan and is an enemy kingdom.

In summary, they:

1. Contend with God's sovereignty by laying claim to creation, dominion, power and wealth (**Ezek 29:3, Ezek. 32:1-2**)

2. Steal kill and destroy (**Jn. 10:10**) through various sins

3. Deceive (**Rev. 12:13**)

4. Make war with saints (**Rev. 12:15, 17; Rev. 13:17**, etc.)

5. Hinder the gospel by using "false prophets" to do evil and many undiscerning people visit these false prophets

6. Rule whole cities, nations or communities by manifesting through political leaders, witchcraft, sorcery and all manners of wickedness.

THE RESPONSE GOD REQUIRES OF US

In the scriptures, God rebuked complacency in the women of Zion. The truth however is that God detests complacency not only in the women, but in His Body in Zion, the Church. "Rise up, you women who are at ease, hear my voice; You complacent daughters, give ear to my speech. In a year and some days you will be troubled, you complacent women; for the vintage will fail, the gathering will not come. Tremble, you women who are at ease; be troubled, you complacent ones; strip yourselves, make yourselves bare, and gird sackcloth on your waists. People shall mourn upon their breasts for the pleasant fields, for the fruitful vine. On the land of my people will come up thorns and briers, yes, on all the happy homes in the joyous city; because the palaces will be forsaken, the bustling city will be deserted. The forts and towers will become lairs forever, a joy of wild donkeys, a pasture of flocks, until the Spirit is poured upon us from on high, and the wilderness becomes a fruitful field, and the fruitful field is counted as a forest." **(Is 32:9-15)**.

From this scripture, we can see that our complacency in controlling our natural environment through intercession leads to many disasters:

"Pleasant fields turn to thorns and briers harvests fail prosperous and bursting cities become deserted desolation (i.e., sin, satanic oppression, occultic influences) takes over cities and even the Church!"

All these begin to manifest until the Spirit is poured down from on high and manifests through informed intercession and spiritual warfare, by God's people and then:

The wilderness becomes a fruitful field, and

The fruitful field enlarges to become like forest

A father in intercession and spiritual warfare, Kjell Sjoberg, put this idea very well into his book, Winning the Prayer War.

God's people, and those who pray, have the keys of a place. If they become slack in intercession, they are like a farmer ceasing to plough and cultivate his field. The evil spirits like weeds are free to grow again and to regain the upper hand. But if God's people maintain their position of victory and take the responsibility for intercession in their area, then they become channels for God's fullness, so that all can testify, "Here, the Lord truly lives among His people."

If we desire to take our cities and nations for God and check the advance of wickedness and abominations around us, so that the kingdoms of this world might become the kingdoms of our God and of His Christ, the church of God needs to become more sensitive and available for God's need for a warrior company of people.

It is only as we yield ourselves to the prophetic and apostolic move of God in these last days that we can conquer our lands for our God.

GOD

By yielding ourselves to be among the warrior company, God will use in these last days; we will be:

1. Breaking bonds of wickedness in our territories and cities (**Is. 58:6**)

2. Setting captives free (**Is. 49:24-26**)

3. Enforcing the manifestation of God's will and purposes (**Eph. 3:10; Rom. 8:19**)

4. Standing in our priestly office (**1 Pet. 2:9**)

5. Repairing and rebinding desolations of many generation and ruined cities (**Is. 61: 4**)

6. Causing God's kingdom to come on earth and His will to be done (**Lk. 11:2**)

7. Causing the veil of darkness over cities and nations to be lifted and destroyed (**Is. 25:7**)

8. Recovering lands the enemy has taken through the ignorance of people and their involvement in idolatry (**Deut. 2:24-25**)

9. Breaking the power of curses and ancient covenants over the lands and the people (**2 Kings 2:19-21**)

WAGING WARFARE AGAINST WATER SPIRITS

The following are ways to wage war against water spirits.

1. Spiritual mapping:

Spiritual mapping can be defined as the discerning of the actual spiritual state of a place or entity through seeing beyond what the place or entity appears to be Daniel Onyechi.

The enemy, Satan, is still the same, but as the warfare against his kingdom heats up, he is also operating in more subtle ways developing inroads and strongholds clandestinely in homes, offices, educational institutions, recreational systems, arts and culture, etc. This is apart from places in our environment where his presence is more obvious.

To do effective warfare against the powers of darkness now, it is important to identify the princes, powers and demons by name, identify their locations, discover the history of their presence in particular locations, identify "happenings" in our environment traceable to particular principalities and powers, etc.

"Every purpose is established by counsel; by wise counsel wage war." (**Prov. 20:18**).

"...but through knowledge the righteous shall be delivered." (**Prov. 11:9b**).

The Bible encourages us to be cautious, *"...lest Satan should take advantage of us; for we are not ignorant of his devices"* (**2 Cor. 2:11**).

Spiritual mapping exposes the enemy preventing him from taking advantage over us. The knowledge we gain from spiritual mapping helps us to do effective warfare so that we will not be like men who "beat the air". (**1 Cor. 9:26b**).

Spiritual mapping information concerning our lives, families, establishments, territories, cities, nations, etc., can be acquired by:

Observation of our natural environment with the gift of discernment of Spirit

*Conducting interviews and asking informed questions about the environment; elders in the environment can be particularly useful (**Job 12:12**)*

Examining books, and other print and media materials

Listening to God in prayers and fasting (**Ps. 25:14; Prov. 25:2**) as you ask the Holy Spirit for information and relevant warfare strategies

2. Personal deliverance from water spirit manifestations:

*Bring repentance for every initiation and dedication, sacrifices made and covenants entered into, vows and marriages contracted with water spirits, worship given to them, etc. (**Is. 59:1,2; 2 Chr. 7:14; Prov. 28:13**).*

*Make atonement through the blood of Jesus, the blood of the new covenant (**Heb. 9:22; Heb. 12:24**).*

Renounce these connections, covenants, dedications divorce all spiritual marriage through initiation and/or dreams.

Break all tokens of satanic covenants you made with the water spirits.

Allow the spirit to be cast out.

*Carry out spiritual warfare against all points of contact and tokens in the sun, moon and stars because the tides are controlled by the moon (**Ps. 21:6-8**).*

WEAPONS OF WARFARE AGAINST WATER SPIRITS

A. The sword of the Lord (Is. 27:1)
B. The hook of the Lord (Ezek. 29:3-5)
C. The mighty arm of the Lord (Ps. 89:10, 13; Job 26:136)
D. The power of Godï¿½s presence (1 Sam. 5:2-4)
E. The blood of Jesus (Rev. 12:11)
F. The weapon of praise (2 Chr. 20)
G. Prophetic declaration into the water (2 Kings 2:19-21)

3. Community Deliverance from Water Spirit Manifestation:

*Corporate fasting and praying to receive divine strategies and scriptures from the Lord (**Josh. 5:13, Josh. 6:5**)*

*Bring corporate identificational repentance for the worship, priesthood, vows and covenants made with the water spirits, etc. (**Neh. 1:4 -11; Dan. 9:3- 19, Ezra 9:1-15**).*

Carry out spiritual warfare with scriptures the Lord lays in your heart while waiting on Him.

Usually, the Lord lays it in the heart of His warriorsto do some prophetic praying and take some prophetic actions.

4. Some prophetic actions the Lord had directed in some previous warfare against water spirits include:

Anointing the waters with anointing oil over which we had prayed

The brethren take communion and pour out the remaining wine of the communion into the waters, symbolic of the blood of Jesus.

Relevant scriptures are written in small pieces of paper and thrown into the waters with prophetic declarations

Some brethren have been led to drop the whole Bible or New Testament Bible alone into some waters with specific proclamations over the waters.

Scriptures are given in some instances to be declared and proclaimed over the waters.

TESTIMONY

There is a river in the city of Ibadan, southwest Nigeria called Ogunpa, which for several years overflows its banks and causes death and wanton destruction of property. In 2001, the Lord led us to begin to pray against the forces operating through the river.

As we prayed, the Lord gave us several strategies including:

Getting some brethren to prayer-walk some portions of the banks of the river

Prophetically changing its name from Ogunpa, a god that kills, to Idunu, a thing of joy

Corporate warfare

Prophetic action of dropping scriptures written on pieces of paper into the river, anointing the river by pouring oil into it, pouring salt into it and taking communion by the river throwing the remaining communion things into the river

Praising and worshiping God thereafter by the river

Since that time, there has been no overflowing of the river and the government has designated a large amount of money for the channeling of the river.

CHAPTER 7

EVIL EFFECTS OF WATER SPIRIT WORSHIP

In this chapter, we wish to examine what happens when people turn their back on the true God and worship other gods:

1. It provokes God's anger.

Worship of water spirits or any other god gets God very angry and provokes Him to release judgment on the people and on the land.

In **Exodus 20:4-5**, God forbids the worship of anything in the waters. He says those who worship them hate Him (see **Judges 2:12; Deut. 31:16-17; Jer. 7:17-20; Num. 25:1-3**).

2. It brings a curse.

The Psalmist said, "*Their sorrow shall be multiplied who hasten after another god*" (**Ps. 16:4**), and "Let all be put to shame who serve carved images...." (**Ps. 97:7**). God says they are cursed.

"*Cursed is the one who makes a carved or molded image, an abomination to the Lord, the works of the hands of craftsmen and sets it up in secret.*" (**Deut. 27:15**).

3. Idolatry attracts war and bloodshed.

Check out the nations of Africa, the wars and bloodshed can be traced to Idolatry and more recently, because of America's involvement in so much of occultism; she has one war or another with other nations (**Jer. 7:31-34; Ezek. 6:13-14**).

4. It delivers the people to captivity and oppression.

God allows oppression in the land and gives the people over to their enemies.

They forsook the Lord and served Baal and the Ashtoreths and the anger of the Lord was hot against Israel, so He delivered them into the hand of plunderers who despoiled them and He sold them unto the hands of their enemies all around, that they could not stand before their enemies (**Judges 2:13-14**).

The Babylonian captivity was all due to the sin of idolatry. In the western world today, even through one can see beautiful houses, cars, roads and other beautiful infrastructure, it is so sad and disheartening the level of oppression of the people.

5. God oppresses the people.

God himself resists and stands against those who are involved in idolatry; He frustrates them.

"Whenever they went out, the hand of the Lord was against them for calamity as the Lord had said and as the Lord had sworn to them. And they were greatly distressed" (**Judges 2:15**).

6. Idolatry defiles and pollutes the land and the people.

God laments that idolatry defiles this land and that He will "Fish out" and "hunt" for idolaters to punish them (**Jer. 16:16-18**).

7. It brings a covering of darkness over the land and the people.

"And He will destroy on this mountain the surface of the covering cast over all people, and the veil that is spread over all nations." (**Is. 25:7**).

8. It affects not only the person that commits the sin but many generations. This is expressly stated in **Exodus 20:1-6**, but an example can be seen in the life of Jeroboam who brought idolatry into Israel and the next 16 kings, no matter how they tried to worship the true God, fell into the sin of idolatry, ultimately including Jehu who had killed Jezebel and others for their idolatry (**2 Kings 10:28-31**).

9. It transfers the land and its resources therein to the control of spirits.

Worship of water spirits is idolatry and we must not only flee from it, we must war against it.

CHAPTER 8

TO DELIVER THE POWER OF GOD

Having done so much exposition of water-spirit manifestation, evil influences, manners of contamination and initiation etc, it is important for us to finish this booklet with a revelation of the power of Jehovah to deliver from these wicked spirits.

There are certain things we must do to allow God accomplish His purposes in our lives, families and nation:

1. HUMBLE YOURSELF

There is a scripture we often quote in praying for our nations, but it is not only for healing of nations. It applies equally to our individual lives and families.

"...if My people who are called by My Name will humble themselves and pray and seek My face and turn from their wicked ways, then I will hear from heaven and will forgive their sin and heal their land." (**2 Chr. 7:14**, emphasis mine).

If we see a manifestation of any of these symptoms, we should humble ourselves and ask for anointed servants of God to pray for us a prayer of deliverance. Thousands have been delivered from the yoke of oppression of water spirits.

2. PRAY

They themselves need to be very prayerful even though the spirits hinder the prayer life of her captives.

But the scriptures say, *"Shall the prey be taken from the mighty or the captives of the righteous be delivered? But thus says the Lord: 'Even the captives of the mighty shall be taken away, and the prey of the terrible be delivered for I will contend with him who contends with you and I will save your children.'"* (**Is. 49:24-25**).

3. SEEK HIS FACE

Ask God questions, and He will give you answers.

"I sought the Lord and He heard me and delivered me from all my fears. They looked to Him and were radiant and their faces were not ashamed." (**Ps. 34:4-5**).

A brother was fed up of a life of continuous struggle with nothing to show for his struggles and efforts in life. As he did seven days of praying and fasting, the Lord ministered to him to ask his father questions.

His father confessed he had been involved in rituals to make him rich, and he was asked by the occultic priest to drop cowrie shells into every river from Nigeria all the way to Ghana in West Africa. He said this was the source of his wealth. By this action, the brother's life had been covenanted to the water spirits.

This was the beginning of the deliverance of this brother from Satan's oppression. (See also, **Hos. 4:6; Is. 5:13-14**).

4. TURN AWAY FROM YOUR WICKED WAYS

There is nothing God can do long as you do not repent of your sins of idolatry.

"Behold, the Lord's hand is not shortened that it cannot save nor His ear heavy that it cannot hear, but your iniquities have separated you from your God and your sins have hidden His face from you so that He will not hear." (**Is. 59:1-2**).

Once there is repentance, admitting and turning away from the sin of idolatry, God begins to move to deliver His children or the nation.

5. ASK FOR AND RECEIVE NEEDED ANOINTING

The power and fire to carry out deliverance of people and places with marine spirits manifestations can be obtained only from God but the good news is that it is yours for the asking.

Meditate on the following scriptures: **Matt. 3:11; Acts 10:38; Lk. 24:49; Ps. 110:1-3; Ps. 144:1, Ps. 85:6, Deut 2:24-25**.

In **Deut. 2:24**, God told the Israelites to go across the River Arnon. He said He has given the king and his land to Israel, but that Israel should begin to possess the land and engage him in battle.

To possess America, Africa and our nations for the Lord, there are spiritual battles to be fought against water spirits, witchcraft, queen of heaven and numerous other satanic forces of darkness, because unwittingly men have given these lands to these forces through idolatrous practices.

The assurance we have is that as we go into these battles, we are not going in our strength and therefore, we have the victory. Meditate on these scriptures: **Rev. 12:11; Col. 2:15; Eph. 6:11-18; Col. 2:13; I Cor. 15:58; Lk. 10:18-19; Ps. 8:6-8; Ps. 91:13; Ps. 51:20-23; Ezek. 22:30-31**.

Let us be as Caleb who said, "*Let us go up at once and take possession for we are well able to overcome it.*" God was well pleased with Joshua and Caleb and because they trusted in Him, they lived and prospered. For those who were fearful, they perished in the wilderness.

BIBLIOGRAPHY

1. The Four Elements: Earth, Air, Fire and Water
-Amanda Buy

2. IdolatryProblems, Principles, Panacea
-Emeka Nwakpa

3. Exposition on Water Spirits
-Victoria Eto

4. Waging War with Knowledge
-Daniel Onyechi

5. Dealing with Idolatry
-Simeon Mbevi

6. Mysterious Secrets of the Dark Kingdom, The Battle for Planet Earth
-J.P. Timmons.

7. Identifying the Dark Force of the Aquatic World
-Samuel K.D. Dikaniakina

8. Winning the Prayer War
-Kjell Sjoberg

All scriptures in this book are from New Kings James version (NKJV) of the Bible, unless otherwise indicated.

Made in the USA
Charleston, SC
09 April 2016